I0467731

HOW TO MAKE YOUR
RETIREMENT
LAST AS LONG AS YOU DO

By: Cody C. Meeks

Copyright © 2016 Cody C. Meeks

All rights reserved.

ISBN: 1519763972
ISBN-13: 978-1519763976

CONTENTS

CHAPTER 1
INTRODUCTION

March 11, 2005. One of the happiest days of my life. You might be thinking that it was my wedding day. Nope, that's June 4th but this day was <u>almost</u> as special! You see On March 11, 2005, my grandparents decided that after 35 years it was finally time for them to retire.

Ione and Melvin Louk laugh together Wednesday at their Garden City home. Ione will be retiring this summer and the two are planning to move to their second home in Lampe, Mo.

Retirement a longtime coming for Louks

If you haven't made the leap into retirement yet, let me give you some advice as to what's going to happen. Traditionally when individuals make this decision, your close family and friends will send out invitations to your not-so-close family and friends. You will enjoy cake, punch and your former employer will most likely give you a gold watch for your dedicated service (ironic because most retirees don't care what time it is anymore).

I say traditionally because that's not always the case. You see for my grandparents, they had been so influential to their community that EVERYONE in the small town of Garden City, KS, wanted to say their goodbyes. In fact, even the local media wanted to cover their story. At my grandparents' retirement party they had two local newspapers, a radio station AND the 6 o'clock news.

The question between each media source remained the same. "Now that the two of you are going to retire, what's next?"

If you're planning on retiring soon – prepare yourself with an answer to this question. Everyone is going to ask!

When my family and I sat down with my grandparents that night to watch the 6 o'clock news, I remember my grandparents response like it was yesterday. They both went silent. They turned and looked at each other. Then turned back to the camera. Almost in unison they responded, "we are going to retire to Branson, MO."

While my grandparents were working they never made a ton of money, but they understood how important it was to spend time together as a family. Each and every year they would load up in their RV and drive 510 miles to a small RV park just outside of Branson, MO, on Table Rock Lake.

For nearly 50 years they returned to the exact same camp grounds and would spend a week during the summer simply enjoying time together and building memories. For my grandparents, their vision of retirement was to finally own a permanent spot they could call home.

Even though neither of them had ever made much money during their working years, they always lived within their means and saved everything they could. Prior to retirement they met numerous times with their financial advisor to make sure they weren't making a mistake.

"Have we really saved enough?"

"Can we actually afford this?"

"Will we still have enough money left over?"

These are common questions that every retiree asks themselves. Because my grandparents had been so frugal with their money during their working years they just wanted that extra bit of reassurance that they could actually purchase their dream home.

July 15, 2005, following the advice of their financial advisor, my grandparents did it. They purchased their own little piece of heaven right on Table Rock Lake outside of Branson, MO.

Prior to their retirement in 2004, my great grandmother was diagnosed with Alzheimer's disease. If you've ever had a family member affected, you'll know that the disease not only affects the individual, it's very difficult on the entire family. Because of the caring nature of my grandma and grandpa, they promised my great grandma and my family that they would be there until the end.

Even though they had always dreamed of spending all their time at their home in Branson, they would keep both homes; and Garden City would be their primary residence up until my great grandmother passed.

Month after month they would drive the 510 miles to come back to Garden City to fulfill their promise. Even though I didn't get to spend as much time with my grandparents, I was proud that their dreams where being fulfilled.

In the time that I was able to see them I could tell that they both had a renewed outlook on life. There was always this glow that radiated from my grandmother.

My grandpa's eyes were no longer bloodshot. His knees no longer crippled him like they did in years past. You could tell by looking at the two of them that they were truly enjoying their retirement.

After 3 short years, it all came to an abrupt halt. In 2008 the financial marketplace was in ruins. Within 45 days markets had retraced nearly 40%. My grandparents have always believed that god will provide, but with that type of loss they were panicked. They called their financial advisor to schedule an appointment to review their retirement plan.

> *"The stock market has gone down 40% in 45 days, how does that affect our retirement?"*

During the meeting their financial advisor gave them the harsh reality. Even though they were diversified and had their money in multiple places, everything was experiencing a major correction.

At that meeting my grandparents discovered 34% of

the money they had stashed away for retirement was gone... All of the years they had been frugal and put money aside was gone... When my grandparents asked their advisor what to do, he told them they only had a few options. Because they needed the money now, and didn't have time to wait for the markets to recover they would have to:

#1) Sell one of the two homes that they own

OR

#2) Go back to work...

When I next saw my grandparents I could tell something was wrong. They were extremely quiet and just didn't have their normal upbeat and energetic attitudes. In private I asked if everything was ok; and my grandma, with a tear in her eyes, told me about their financial situation.

I was outraged! How could two people that had given so much to others be treated like this? Those couldn't be their only options, there has to be something that can help them! You can't ask someone to choose between fulfilling a promise to their family or selling their dream home. I can't believe their advisor even said that! My grandparents were 69 and 67 years old. When they decided to retire, every news outlet in the city covered their story. He can't ask them to go back to work! Is he serious? These can't be their only options...

During this time in 2008 I was completing my 2nd year in college with the goal to graduate and become an engineer. Because I am a numbers guy, I instantly started researching the financial tools available. There has to be something out there that can save my grandparents...

I became obsessed. I spent every minute I could researching past performance, rates of returns, volatility, standard deviations, anything I could get my hands on relating to investments; I wanted to learn.

As I was doing this I started to classify different investment tools into different categories, each of which had a different purpose. It started to become clear to me, retirement is like a puzzle. There are hundreds of pieces all of which have to fit together to give you a completed picture.

> *"Retirement planning is like a puzzle. There are hundreds of pieces and they all have to fit together to form the complete picture."*

The more I learned, the more I became frustrated with how the advisor had invested my grandparent's assets. Why did he do that? Why were they invested in this? Why were they taking so much risk?

Cody C. Meeks

CHAPTER 2
CAPTIVE VS INDEPENDENT

As I continued to search for answers, I turned my attention away from the investment tools and focused on the advisor. He had to have known how much RISK he was taking with my grandparents' money. Why didn't he invest their money differently since he KNEW they needed that money to provide them income...

"Why did this man, that my grandparents trusted, invest THEIR money the way that he did?"

I began researching the firm in which he worked for because ultimately that is who he must report to. While reading a blog dedicated to the firm in which this individual advisor worked for, I noticed something interesting. In 2008 everyone invested with this company lost about the same percentage as my grandparents. Obviously people with more money lost more, but the percentages where almost identical. I remember myself thinking, how can everyone experience the same losses if they are all working with different advisors in different parts of the country.

> *"Why did everyone that was invested with the same company as my grandparents lose about the same percentage?"*

In the blog I requested that anyone who was willing to please send me information regarding the different vehicles in which they were invested. At first, no one sent me anything, but then they started piling in. Comment after comment was being posted. In the end I had 47 people willing to share their information with me.

From these comments I compiled a master spreadsheet that highlighted their individual investment holdings inside of their accounts. I was merely 10 statements in when I noticed something. Every single person, regardless of how old they were. Regardless of what part of the country they were from. Regardless of how much money they had. All of their portfolios contained two primary investment tools. Mutual funds and Stocks.

> *Every individual held two primary investment tools:*
> - *Stocks*
> - *Mutual Funds*

As I continued to dig, I realized not only did everyone contain the same two investment vehicles, but the internal workings of these vehicles were the same as well. Everyone that was willing to share their information with me was holding the exact same mutual fund!

At this point I realized this wasn't the advisors' fault for my grandparents losing money, it was the company's fault! He only invested their money how the company told him to invest it!

> *He invested my grandparents' money the way his COMPANY wanted him to, not how my grandparents NEEDED it invested...*

But that only raised another question. Why would a company that claims they "personalize" every portfolio for your unique situation and needs require their advisors to invest in a certain way?

This question kept me up at night. It just didn't make sence to me. Why would a company require their advisors to use specific mutual funds?

The answer came to me when I was reading the financial disclosure for this mutual fund. You see every company is required to provide disclosures on the different investment tools that their advisors use. If you look hard enough, these disclosures actually tell the client what is inside of the tool, how it works. It even discloses what they are paying in fees per year.

Unless you have a law degree, these disclosure documents are almost impossible to understand but I was only looking for the advisors compensation. I spent weeks combing through these documents and compiling a master list of all the important details. It seemed to me like the compensation to the advisor was fairly consistent regardless of what they recommended. There has to be a reason. It is not by sheer coincidence that so many people are invested in an identical fashion.

Then I found it!

I was looking in the wrong place. You see, it wasn't listed in the disclosure documents. The disclosure documents are only required to disclose the fees paid for owning that specific investment. It is not required to disclose the fee paid from the carrier or investment tool to the advisor. In a completely separate document, I discovered what is termed as "Revenue Sharing."

I would not be surprised if this is a brand new term to you. Most investors have never been told what it is OR how it works because legally they are not required to tell you about it! Even though these brokerage houses don't have to legally tell you about it, they are now required to publish the document on the firm's website.

So, what is revenue sharing and why do I bring it up?

Revenue Sharing by definition is, *"the distribution of a portion of revenues back to its representatives."*

To put this into language everyone can understand, it's the kick back of profits to specific firms that represent their products. It's the increase in commissions if you represent their investment tools. Here is the language directly from the company's disclosure my grandparents were invested in.

"_____ receives payments known as revenue sharing from certain mutual fund companies, 529 plan program managers and insurance companies (collectively referred to as "product partners"). Virtually all of _____s transactions relating to mutual funds, 529 plans and insurance products involve product partners that pay revenue sharing to _____. We want you to understand that _____s receipt of revenue sharing payments creates a potential conflict of interest in the form of additional financial incentive and financial benefit to the firm, its advisors and equity owners in connection with the sale of products from these product partners. For the year ended December 31st, 2014, _____ received revenue sharing payments of approximately $153.2 million from mutual fund and 529 product partners and $55.9 million from insurance product partners. For the same period, _____s' net income was $770 million."

Let me explain what that disclosure is actually saying. In 2014 the company that was responsible for the financial safety of my grandparents received $209.1 million dollars in excess of the normal commissions paid to the advisor/company. For the same year their NET INCOME as a company was only $770 million. That means that 27% of their total profits were made through "Revenue Sharing."

27% of their TOTAL profits were made through

Revenue Sharing!

Now I'm extremely upset. This company has the nerve to say *"receipt of revenue sharing payments creates a potential conflict of interest in the form of additional financial incentive and financial benefit?"* Over ¼ of the companies' profits are through these kickbacks. That doesn't present a "potential" conflict of interest it is a COMPLETE conflict of interest!

When I finally put these two pieces of the puzzle together I called my grandmother to let her know what I had discovered. "Grandma, your advisor doesn't invest your money how you want it to be invested, he invests it how the company tells him to invest it!"

My grandma, being the person that she is, doesn't see negatives in anyone. She gave me her typical response, "Well he's doing the best he can, everyone lost money in 2008. It's not his or the company's fault"

> *"Everyone lost money in 2008,*
>
> *it's not our advisors fault"*

Even though my grandma didn't clearly understand my frustration, I can't move on and simply chalk it up to the fact that "everyone lost money in 2008". My grandparents had trusted this man for 20+ years. How could he have the audacity to sit across the table from them and say he's investing in their best interests when obviously he's not. He's only putting them in investments that are in his best interest!!!

After the conversation with my grandma I had to step back for a second. What if I'm wrong? Could it be possible that the advisor simply didn't know? Does he even receive extra money from this "revenue sharing" that I had discovered?

Turns out I was wrong...The advisor my grandparents placed their trust in actually receives hardly any of the additional kickbacks. In fact, nearly 100% goes to cooperate and private investors of the firm. My grandma was right. He was doing the best he could to listen to their needs and invest their money. The problem was that the firm he worked for handcuffed him and only allowed him to use certain products that were in THEIR best interest.

With this discovery I wanted to find out if this was the case for all financial advisors. Is everyone only looking out for themselves? In the mainstream retail world I found this to be consistent with basically every brokerage house out there.

Don't believe me? Try this.

If you are currently using a brokerage firm, give them a call and ask to see their "revenue sharing disclosure." By law they are only required to show you this document if you directly ask for it. After the advisor on the other end of the phone gets over the shock that you know what to ask for, have them send it to you.

> *If you are currently with a broker, call them and ask to see their "Revenue Sharing Disclosure"*

I found that some firms are worse than others, but for the most part recommendations were made strictly because of which companies were willing to pay revenue sharing and which wouldn't.

While in college I stumbled upon a company that worked within the financial industry that claimed to represent independent advisors. This was a term I had never heard before so naturally I was curious. It turns out my research on the big brokerage firms was accurate. Ultimately the company controls what products or tools their advisors are allowed to use. The term "independent" means that these advisors have broken away from the "parent" company and are no longer handcuffed by what they can and can't offer to their clients. The independent advisor truly acts as a fiduciary and only cares about the concerns and objectives of their clients.

In 2009, after almost a full year of research in the financial industry, I learned why my grandparents, and many others in their position, had never heard of an independent advisor and had chosen to go with a more "reputable" company.

> *What is an "independent" financial advisor and how are they different from "captive" advisors?*

Being independent from the big firms meant these financial advisors are actually small business owners. They pay for their own marketing, their own office space, and their own staff. Everything required to conduct business, they must pay for out of their own pockets. This means they don't have the money to buy huge billboards, advertise during the super bowl, or sponsor a NASCAR driver.

Which would you rather have, an advisor that is told how to invest your money or an advisor that only cares how YOU want to invest your money?

CHAPTER 3
HIDDEN FEES

In the previous chapter I discussed revenue sharing as a form of additional payment to the financial advisory firm that represents said products, but where does that money come from?

The simple answer – You, the clients that are placing your hard earned money into these vehicles.

Fees have always been a part of everyday life. Ever since commerce was formed people have traded with each other for goods and services. Back in the day if you wanted a goat it would cost you 6 loaves of bread and 2 chickens.

Today if you want a gallon of milk, the store is going to charge you $2.99 (plus the governments share).

Personally, as long as you get something of equal value in exchange for the fee that you pay, then the fee is justified. Individuals that take on the responsibility of managing your assets should be compensated for their ability to provide you a service.

What I don't agree with is someone saying they are going to charge you $2.99 for a gallon of milk, you pay the $2.99, and then when you get to the end of the year and look at the receipt you notice you actually paid $5.99 for that gallon of milk.

> *How can a gallon of milk cost $2.99 but you end up paying $5.99?*

You see, when you purchased the milk you saw the advertised price, but what wasn't disclosed was the fact you would have to pay the transportation fee for getting the milk to the store. The store also charges a fee to place the milk on the store shelf. Don't forget, there is a convenience fee because you purchased from the store and didn't have to go to the cow and get it yourself!

Fees, fees, and MORE fees!!!

Yes, I'm being a bit extreme, but this is how the financial industry gets away with taking YOUR money! They advertise a set fee amount traditionally represented as a percent based on the money you have invested with the firm. You will pay this amount, but what they don't tell you is all of the additional "backend" fees you will be charged.

Don't believe me? Take out the disclosure documents that were provided to you when you opened your accounts. If you have a magnifying glass and 6 hours of free time to scan through the documents you'll find these additional fees I'm talking about.

I was recently working with a couple named Pete & Sarah. The two of them had attended one of my educational workshops, and they didn't believe me about all of the fees companies are allowed to charge. He stated numerous times that he had examined all of the disclosure statements, and they were only paying $40 per year in fees. I told the two of them to book an appointment and bring in the statements and we would call the investment company directly and figure out exactly what they were paying per year.

When they came in we hopped on the phone together with the company, and I started asking the representative on the other end of the phone line a few questions.

Are there fees being charged to my client?

- Yes sir, they currently have a $40 per year administration charge.

You should have seen the smile on Pete's face. He was grinning from ear to ear because he had just proven me wrong.

OK, thank you. Are they paying an administration fee on these accounts?

- Yes sir, they currently a 1% administration fee.

When the representative said that Pete was paying 1% in administration fees I thought Pete was going to break my phone! He jumped from his chair and said, "what do you mean I'm paying 1%?"

I asked Pete to sit back down and I would explain what all of this means once I finished the call.

I continued my conversation with the representative by asking if there are any additional riders on these accounts that he is paying a fee for?

- No sir, there is not an income rider or a death benefit rider attached.

Is there an M&E fee being charged?
- Yes sir, there is a 1% per year M&E fee.

Are there any additional fees on these accounts I haven't asked about?

- Yes, there is a sub account fee of 1.5% per year

When I hung up the phone and turned to Pete and Sarah the smile was gone. It had been replaced with a look of confusion. On the scrap paper that I had been taking notes I calculated their total fees.

Admin Charge = $40 / year

Admin Fee = 1%

M&E Fee = 1%

Income Rider Fee = 0%

Death Ben Rider Fee = 0%

Sub-Account Fee = 1.5%

Total Fees = 3.5% + $40 / year

Turns out Pete & Sarah where paying 3.5% per year in fees. Based on their portfolio of $324k they were being charged $11,340 per year! That's $945 per month! By the way, that's on top of the $40 the company had told them they were paying in fees.

Like I said earlier, I'm not against paying fees as long as you get something of equal value in return. This particular client thought they were only paying $40 per year and they had had these investments for 10 years. Pete & Sarah thought they had paid $400 TOTAL. Turns out over the 10 years they had paid just over $100,000 in FEES! I asked them point blank, have you received $100,000 worth of service?

> *Pete and Sarah thought they had paid $400 TOTAL in Fees, turns out they had paid OVER $100,000!*

Pete's answer, "HECK NO! I didn't feel like I was even getting the $40 per year worth of service, that's why I came to see you!"

Unfortunately individuals walk into our office daily that have no clue what they own, what they are being charged or what their true performance is. In the financial industry as long as it's written somewhere, most of the time in a document written by a lawyer that you can't even understand, it doesn't have to be verbally disclosed.

It is extremely important that you know EXACTLY how much you are paying in fees as it has a MAJOR impact on the overall growth of your accounts over time.

On the next page there is a chart that represents how the average fees paid for different investment options will affect your growth potential over a 10 year period. Each line represents a 5% annual growth rate minus the annual fee which is represented in the legend to the right of the graph.

According to a recent article published in Forbes Magazine by Ty Bernicke titled "The Real Cost of Owning A Mutual Fund." individuals on average pay 4.17% per year in fees by owning a mutual fund! Average cost of owning a variable annuity according to Kaplan in her Forbes article titled "9 Reasons You Need To Avoid Variable Annuities" was 3.5%!

The average fee for a managed portfolio is typically 1.25% and a 401(k) typically charges 0.94% in annual fees.

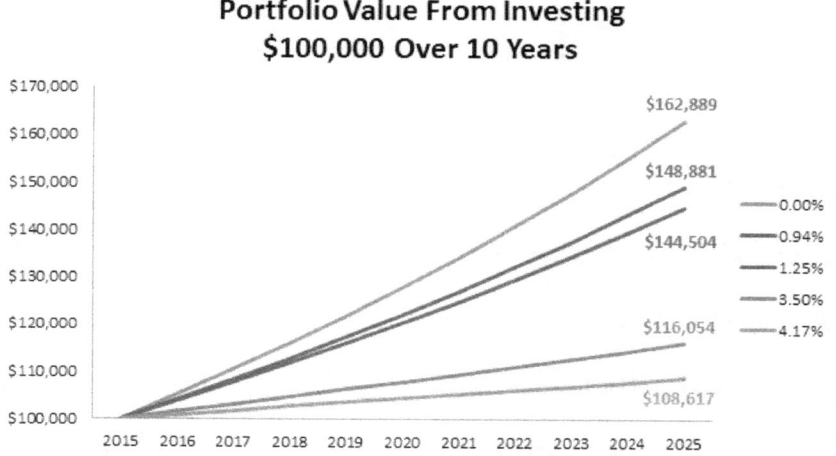

Like I said earlier, I believe that fees are justified as long as you receive equal value to the amount you are paying.

What this graph illustrates is how important it is to know exactly how much you are paying as the amount has a significant impact on the overall growth of your accounts. The difference from paying a 3.5% fee and an account that charges you 0% fee equals a $45,000 difference over ten years.

> *The difference between paying 3.5% in fees vs. 0%*
>
> *in fees over 10 years = $45,000*

You might be saying to yourself, $45,000 is A LOT of money in just 10 years, but there is not an investment out there that I can place my money into that I don't have to pay fees. Trust me, there are investments that have NO fees AND can still provide you a reasonable rate of return.

> *If you are looking for an investment that has 0%*
>
> *fees but still provides you a reasonable rate of*
>
> *return - Call our office to learn more*

Another reason that it's important to know how much you are paying in fees is because you pay them whether you have positive performance OR negative performance within your portfolio. That means, that in good years, the fees are only subtracted from your earnings.　You make money, you just don't make as much.

In years of negative performance, they COMPOUND your losses.　This means that not only did you lose money, but you were then changed a fee which brought your accounts even lower.

Example:

Let's assume a 2% annual fee for the below analysis.

Positive Performance:

Up 10% - 2% (Fee) = **8% annual return**

Up 7% - 2% (Fee) = **5% annual return**

Up 4% - 2% (Fee) = **2% annual return**

Pretty straight forward right? But what happens when we have a negative year?

Negative Performance:

Down 10% + 2 (Fee) = **12% LOSS**

Down 7% + 2% (Fee) = **9% LOSS**

Down 4% + 2% (Fee) = **6% LOSS**

So in a negative year not only do you lose money, but the advisor still gets paid out of YOUR pocket!

Do you know what that reminds me of? Picture this, you decide to have a date night. You hire a baby sitter to come over and watch the kids. You enjoy a nice meal, go to a movie, come back and find out that one of your kids is missing! When you left you had 4 kids, now you have 3. Some of you might ask, "well which one is missing?" Most are going to be furious with the baby sitter, panic, and start looking for the missing child. Let me ask, would you ever hire that babysitter again?

> *If the babysitter lost one of your children, would you hire them again?*

The financial advisor is the babysitter. Not only did they lose part of your money (your child) but you hired them to try again next year AND you still paid them their fee when they lost your child!

Obviously if you are invested in the stock market, you're going to have ups and downs. Since no one can predict the future no advisor is going to be right 100% of the time. What I am trying to educate you on is making sure that you don't let the fees compound your losses at times when your advisor is incorrect.

The example I gave you previously with the client paying $11,340 per year is typical for what walks into my office. In fact, I rarely have a client sit down with me who is paying less than 3% per year. Don't own something that you don't know how much it costs!

> *You know how much a gallon of gas costs.*
> *You know how much a loaf of bread costs.*
>
> *Do you truly know EXACTLY how much your investments cost?*

If you want, call my office and we'll setup a time to discuss EXACTLY what it is that you own and find out how much you are REALLY paying in fees.

Cody C. Meeks

BUILDING <u>YOUR</u> RETIREMENT PLAN

Cody C. Meeks

CHAPTER 4

GENERATING INCOME

Although I don't believe in a universal plan for every client that has chosen to partner with our firm, I do believe that every plan contains the same components. For us, it all begins with income. I define retirement as becoming permanently unemployed. Isn't that the goal? Don't you want to leave your job behind and spend the rest of your life on a paid vacation?

My job is to convert what you've saved in your nest egg into that "paid" vacation.

Even though we all go to work and claim to love what we do, most of us wouldn't show up if we weren't getting paid. With that said I think it's safe to assume you went to work in order to gain an income. If you are fortunate, you might have a pension from your current employer which we will talk about, but for most of us that paycheck is gone the day we leave.

Because the paychecks stop, but the cost of living doesn't, we have to replace that income. I consider this step of the plan the most crucial. If you underestimate your expenses, or use an investment to generate income that is not guaranteed, you could be faced with hard decisions in retirement like my grandparents faced.

If you've ever had a financial advisor tell you that your expenses are going to be less in retirement, he obviously doesn't specialize with pre-retirees/retirees. Don't believe me, ask yourself this question. Do you spend more money Monday – Friday when you are at work or do you spend more Saturday – Sunday when you have spare time and you want to enjoy doing something unique and different.

> *Most retirees underestimate the expenses and the amount they will spend on entertainment during retirement.*

During retirement, not only will you have the everyday expenses you have currently; electric bill, water bill, car insurance, etc. You are going to have to pay your own health insurance, and you will more than likely have an increase in recreational expenses. For most of the clients that I work with, their required income is equal to if not MORE in retirement than when they were working.

The first part of my process is to analyze your monthly expenses and develop a written budget so that we can correctly solve how much income you are going to need.

> ~ 57% of pre-retirees underestimate their expenses during retirement according to an article published in the Journal of Accountancy by Vein, C. Titled "More than half of clients underestimate their retirement expenses."

Once we have determined how much you truly need on a monthly basis, we can then figure out how much of that income will be generated from outside sources such as Social Security and Pensions.

> ~ 72% of retirees will rely on Social Security as their primary income source according to www.ss.gov

Most of us will be eligible to receive Social Security benefits but very few potential clients understand the filing strategies they can take advantage of to maximize their payments.

In fact, I yet to have someone sit down with me in the first appointment that had a written plan on how to maximize their Social Security benefits.

If you are in this situation, call my office and I'll run a free report that will help you maximize your benefits. You've already paid into Social Security your entire life, why wouldn't you want to get the most you can back out of the program?

Since so many of you reading this book are going to rely on Social Security for a significant portion of your financial income plan, we will develop a strategy to maximize those benefits and replace any income lost in the event that one spouse passes away before the other.

This is another common mistake I see in regards to income planning. You and your spouse file for Social Security, you're collecting your benefits, you may be lucky enough to have a pension – but then your spouse dies. What happens now?

Let me show you how this might impact your financial security.

Recently I had a couple named Dennis and Carol who wanted to make sure their income was going to be ok if one of them passed before the other. This was a huge concern to Dennis because his first wife had already passed away, and he knew firsthand the impact it had on his finances, and he wanted to make sure that would never happen to Carol.

When I sat with Dennis and Carol they both had already turned on their Social Security benefits. Dennis was receiving $1800 and Carol was collecting $1000. From his former employer Dennis was fortunate enough to receive a pension of $1200 per month.

	Social Security	Pension
Dennis	$1,800	$1,200
Carol	$1,000	

Total = $4,000 / month

Between the two of them they were collecting $4,000 per month which was adequate. They had no debt. They lived a modest lifestyle but didn't need much outside of day to day expenses. The only thing they really enjoyed doing with their money was traveling.

When I started to review their financial situation I noticed a few red flags that neither of them had considered. If Dennis would pass before Carol, she would instantly lose $1,000 a month from her Social Security. The Social Security rules state that as a married couple when one spouse dies you keep the larger of the two benefits, you do NOT keep both benefits.

What I also noticed was that when Dennis elected his pension payout he choose to elect a single lifetime payout. I asked Dennis if he remembered making that selection when he filed for his pension. His response was that he elected the pension payments right after his first wife had passed to help him recoup what was lost during her passing. He wasn't married to anyone and didn't expect to remarry so he took the single payment option.

In looking at the numbers, IF Dennis where to pass away before Carol, she would not only have the emotional strain of losing her partner in life, she would also lose over 50% of her monthly income!

	Social Security	Pension
Dennis	$1,800	$1,X00
Carol	$1,X00	

Total = $4,X00 / month

$1,800 / month

Retirees face many unique challenges specific to retirement which is why you need to partner with someone that specializes in this time period of your life. You've never been in retirement before; you don't know what to expect or what to plan for.

With proper planning Dennis and Carols' situation was corrected BEFORE it became a major problem. I noticed the issue and solved in today's dollars how much they needed to set aside and invest to generate the $2700 a month that Carol would need if/when Dennis predeceased her.

We cannot prevent Dennis from passing away, but we can prevent the financial heartbreak that goes along with losing your spouse.

Cody C. Meeks

CHAPTER 5

CREATING AN EMERGENCY FUND

After we develop a plan to create a guaranteed income stream for both you and your spouse that you cannot outlive AND we make sure it is sufficient to cover all day to day expenses, we have to set money aside for the unexpected.

Everyone has their raining day fund. The money that you set somewhere safe, make sure it's liquid to protect you in case something unexpected happens. Say the hot water heater breaks or you have to make an unexpected trip to see your brand new grandchild. You have to plan that from time to time you are going to have some expenses that are not within your typical monthly budget.

Most clients place this money in a savings account at the bank although I have had clients stuff it under their mattress.

To me, it doesn't matter where you store this money as long as the vehicle has two very important properties.

```
#1 – Is it Safe?
```

What do I mean when I ask is it safe? What I am asking is the principal 100% guaranteed? If you put $50,000 into your emergency fund and your car breaks down, is there still $50,000 left in the account. An emergency fund has to be there WHEN you need it, not IF you need it.

```
#2 – Is it Liquid?
```

When I ask is it liquid what I'm asking is how hard is it for you to access? If you needed the money tomorrow, could you get it?

Personally I don't think hiding money under your mattress is a good place to have your emergency fund, but I understand why some have it there. In fact, with today's low interest rates at the bank the money you have under the mattress is getting basically the same return that you would at the bank!

Because we've had these historically low interest rates for so long, I often get asked, is there a better place to put my emergency fund than the bank? When I hear my clients ask me that question what they are actually asking is:

#1. I need a safe place for my money

#2. I need it to be 100% liquid

#3. I want to get a decent interest rate on my money

If you are reading this and have these same concerns, call my office and schedule an appointment because we have found an investment vehicle that meets all three of those concerns and provides clients a reasonable rate of return.

> *"It's not the return ON my money I'm interested in, it's the return OF my money..."*
>
> *~ Mark Twain*

CHAPTER 6

SAFE ACCUMULATION

During our working years we focus on two common areas when it comes to the assets we set aside for retirement.

First, how much can we afford to save/put back in an account ear marked for retirement.

Second, how can we invest that money so that it grows rapidly and we have much more than what we actually put in.

To financial professionals, this phase of your life is called the accumulation phase. When you are in the accumulation phase your only focus is on how large you can grow your retirement nest egg.

> *Accumulation Phase = Working Years*
>
> *#1. How much can you save?*
>
> *#2. How fast can you grow it?*

Because you don't intend on accessing or needing this money until you retire, you're able to take much greater risk knowing that you have TIME to wait out negative market performance.

Many of us start saving for retirement when we get our first "real" job. Typically between the ages of 25 and 30. Since most individuals don't retire until their mid-60's we are conditioned to believe we need to continue this accumulation trend throughout retirement. This often means that when I sit with individuals getting ready to enter retirement they are still taking the same RISK within their portfolio as they did when they were 35 or 40 years old.

It's really no surprise to me though. If you've never been retired before, you don't know how or what you should be doing. I also find that most of the pre-retirees I meet with are still using the same advisor they did when they were in the 40's and 50's. As you enter retirement, it's important that you find a financial professional that specializes in retirement planning. The entire investment philosophy changes as you leave the accumulation phase and enter the next phase of your life which is called the distribution phase.

Think of it this way. When you were young, you went to a pediatrician because they specialize in ailments that affect children. As you grew into a young adult did you keep going to the pediatrician? If you needed to have heart surgery would you go to your family doctor? NO, in all aspects of your life you want to find a specialist. Retirement planning is no different.

The financial advisor that you choose to partner with during your working years specialized in growing your assets. I am guessing they have probably done a pretty good job for you up until this point in accomplishing this task or you wouldn't still be using them. As you leave the accumulation phase of your life and enter the distribution phase, you can no longer take as much RISK because you don't have the luxury of TIME to wait out negative market performance.

During the distribution phase we convert your nest egg that you've accumulated throughout your working life into monthly distributions to pay for your living expenses.

> *Distribution Phase = Retirement*
>
> *Turn your nest egg into paychecks*

What is the most crucial component of the distribution phase?

You can only take a distribution from something that is there! If you suffer a loss from the stock market and you need to withdraw money to pay your electric bill, you can't wait until the market goes back up. TIME is no longer on your side...

As we discussed in chapter 4, when I develop a retirement plan I have already solved for paying the "non-negotiable" expenses using guaranteed income investments. If you remember, I classify "non-negotiable" expenses as the day to day costs of living. Meaning, you have to pay your house payment or the bank will take your house from you. You have to pay your electric bill or you won't have electricity. If you develop your plan the way I have laid out in this book where you have a GUARANTEED income stream, and an emergency account, the money you have left over will be placed into your "safe-accumulation" bucket.

In your safe-accumulation bucket you can afford to take slightly more risk, but never the amount of risk that you were taking while you were working. You could have something truly unexpected happen that depletes your entire emergency fund so you have to make sure this money is there WHEN you need it, not IF you need it.

I'm often asked, could I leave this portion of my money in the stock market?

The simple answer is yes, but I must elaborate; and I will refer back to my specialist analogy. If you choose to leave this portion of your money in the stock market, you need to find a professional that focuses on SAFE asset allocation. This will typically NOT be the advisor that you've worked with up until this point in time.

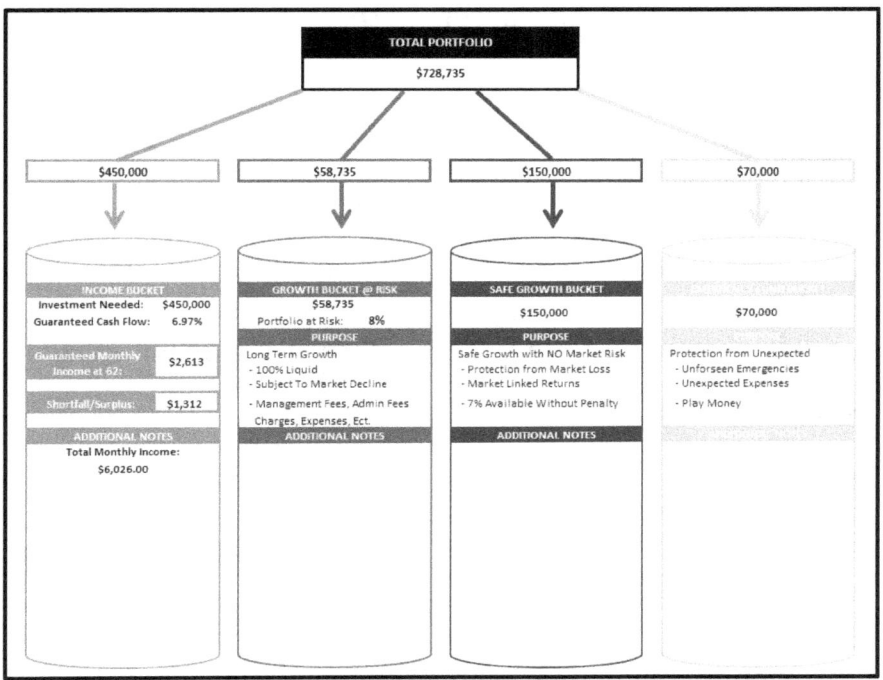

Above is how I construct what I call the "Complete Financial Plan." We have solved for your income needs on a GUARANTEED basis. We've placed a portion of your assets into an emergency bucket for unexpected expenses. We then fund a bucket specifically designed to provide upside potential WITHOUT downside risk which I call the safe accumulation bucket.

My clients understand the importance of having their money available WHEN they need it. Yes, some do leave a portion of their assets in the stock market but for a majority of them they don't want to wake up in the middle of the night wondering IF their money is still there or not.

Have you ever heard the phrase, losses hurt you more than gains?

That's not just a phrase; it's 100% true. Because of how math works, losses truly do hurt you much more than gains.

Let me explain. If you are in the stock market and you have $100,000 invested. During the 1st year your portfolio experiences a loss of 15%. This means that your $100,000 is no longer worth $100,000. It's now only worth $85,000.

$100,000 – 15% Loss = $85,000

If any of you were invested in the stock market in 2008, you know the reality of losing money all too well...

Let's say that in the following year the markets recover. Your portfolio experiences a 15% gain. Is your account now worth $100,000 like it was when you started?

$$\$85,000 + 15\% \text{ Gain} = \$97,750$$

You might be asking yourself, how can this be? I lost 15%, I gained 15%, I should be back to even right?

Because you experienced a loss BEFORE your account had the gain, you had less money for the gain to be applied to. We call this the Sequence of Returns. Simply put, if you experience a loss, it will require a larger gain to bring you back to even.

If you had experienced the 15% loss in the above

example, it would actually take just over 17.6% for your accounts to be worth $100,000 again.

$$\boxed{\$85,000 + 17.6\% \text{ Gain} = \$99,960}$$

The chart below illustrates how the Sequence of Returns can affect your retirement account. IF you would have experienced the 34% loss to your accounts like my grandparents did in 2008 it would have taken almost 54% for them to be back to EVEN!

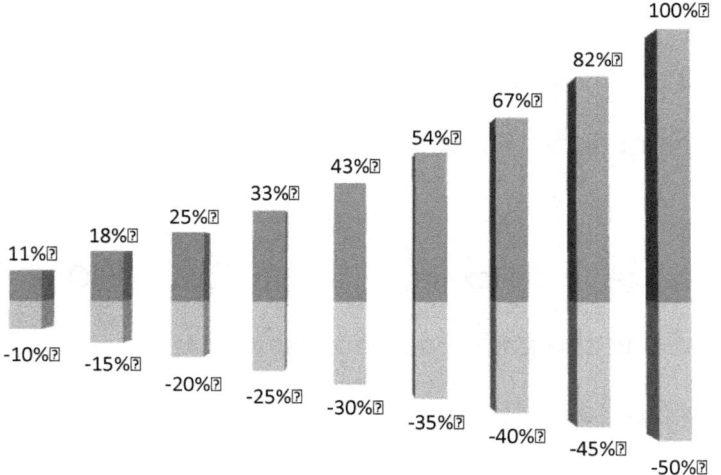

Sequence of Returns

A 35% loss would need

A 54% gain to break EVEN!

Another important rule for us to remember when it comes to your investments is the difference between AVERAGE return and ACTUAL return. When you have the conversation with your current advisor about how your accounts have performed, you will often be told, "your accounts have AVERAGED _____% over the past 10 years that you've had them invested with me."

Average is not the same as actual and let me show you what I mean.

If we take the same $100,000 we used in the previous example and we apply a 100% gain to the account. Yes, I know 100% gain is not realistic but it will make the math easier to understand.

After our $100,000 has gained 100%, its now with $200,000 correct?

$100,000 + 100% Gain = $200,000

Because we gained 100% in 1 year, we are obviously in a very volatile stock, but you left it in there hoping to have another good year. Unfortunately, this year the stock went down 50%

$200,000 - 50% Loss = $100,000

The math is pretty simple, but here is where I show you that average returns don't matter. If you were to look at your investments, you made 100% in the first year and lost 50% in the next year; and you were in that investment for two years. If we were to do the math, your AVERAGE rate of return was 25%.

Year 1 = 100% Gain

Year 2 = 50% Loss

Total Return = 50%

You owned it for 2 years = 25% Average / year

Your actual rate of return was 0%. You started with $100,000 and you finished with $100,000. Which do you care more about? The 25% average per year that your advisor tells you about, or the actual return which says you only have $100,000 which is exactly where you started?

Hopefully I have explained these two examples clearly enough that you understand the importance of WHEN you experience gains and losses and ACTUAL vs. AVERAGE rates of returns. In both examples the problem was not the gain. We love when our accounts go up in value. It was the loss that affected us the most.

So, is there a way that you can still participate in the upside of the market but eliminate your losses?

Actually there is an investment vehicle available that allows you to trade part of the good to eliminate the bad. When I say that what I mean is there is an investment vehicle out there that protects you 100% from any negative performance of the stock market.

If you put in $100,000 and the markets go down 10%, your $100,000 is still worth $100,000.

Obviously if someone else protects you from experiencing a loss to your accounts, they have to have some form of compensation or there would be no reason for them to do it. Like I said, this investment works by trading ALL of the losses for a PORTION of the gains.

For example, one of the investments that I use frequently in my office allows you to "participate" in stock market performance. What they mean is when the stock market goes down, you lose nothing. When it goes up you participate in those gains by a percentage that the company declares. The vehicle that I use currently allows you to participate in 50% of the upside.

Example:

> Year 1: Down 10% = You lose NOTHING
>
> Year 2: Up 10% (you get 50% of the 10%)
>
> $\qquad$ = a 5% gain or $105,000

Often I'm asked, why would I put my money in an investment that limits my upside? Remember our previous examples. Depending on WHEN you experience a loss is much more important because all we care about is the ACTUAL return, not the AVERAGE. By eliminating the losses you never have to "chase old money" or play "catch up" to get back to even. Whenever the market is up, you go up with it. When it goes down, you stay right where you were.

Below is a real life example of what this looks like using REAL returns, not hypothetical. This compares one of the investments that I use vs. the ACTUAL S&P 500 returns.

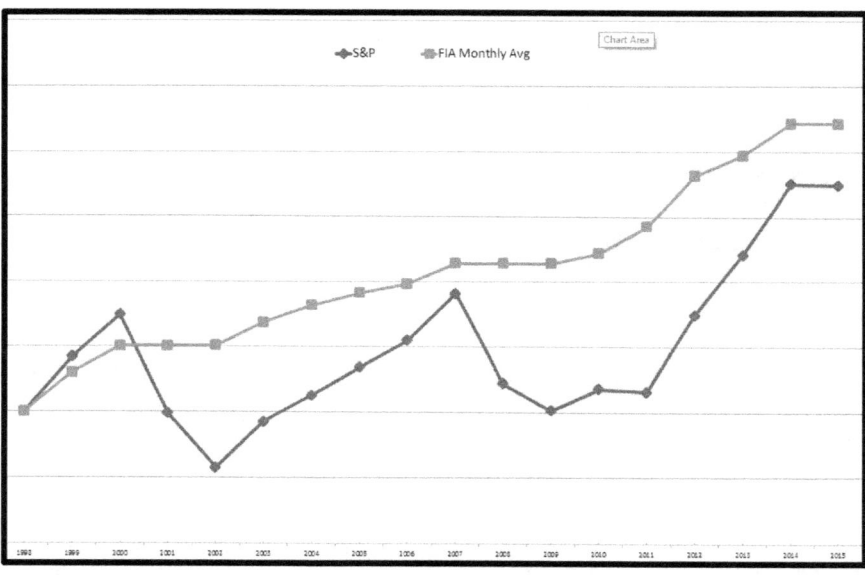

Even though these investments were never designed to "beat" the stock market performance, because they never experience a loss in value when the stock market goes down they actually can and have outperformed the stock market!

(The above graph is from Sept 30th 1998 – Sept 30th 2015)

When potential clients sit down and tell me they are concerned about losing money in the next stock market correction, I joke with them and ask when they think the correction is coming? My crystal ball hasn't been working so well. I thought the correction was going to happen 3 years ago!

I know that losing money is not a joking matter, but it doesn't have to be that way. Your retirement success does not have to be based on the ability of your financial advisor "predicting" what the stock market is going to do...

> Is your retirement success based on the ability of your financial advisor "predicting" what the stock market is going to do?

The reason I use investment options in which a client can never lose money is because I want to GUARANTEE your retirement success. I don't want to leave your success to chance!

Cody C. Meeks

CHAPTER 7

PROVIDING A LEGACY

Legacy, the last part of my financial plan. Ultimately most people want to leave behind a portion of their wealth. Whether that be to support their favorite charity or maybe they are wanting to give it to their children. Often times, when I sit down with a client they tell me they REALLY want to leave something behind, but they have no clue how to do it. They don't understand the most efficient ways of leaving money behind. They don't know how much they can afford to leave behind. The reason that I leave legacy till the end of my planning process is because if done properly to this point, determining how much you can afford to leave behind is simple.

> Your INCOME is GUARANTEED.
>
> You have an EMERGENCY fund for the unexpected.
>
> You have an account for SAFE GROWTH.

By going through the complete planning process and forming each of these individual accounts with a specific purpose, it provides retirees the peace of mind that all their bases are covered. Whatever is left over, if there is anything left over, we can structure to leave a legacy.

What I just discussed is the positive form of leaving a legacy, which you may or may not be able to afford. I haven't yet discussed the other side of leaving behind a legacy. The last thing you want to be thinking about as you pass on is what the negative effects will be on your family after you die.

Is your spouse going to take a significant income

reduction?

Is your family going to have to pay for your final expenses?

Whatever assets you have remaining, are they structured to pass to your beneficiaries tax free or are they going to have to pay taxes on everything?

Even though legacy is the last step in my financial journey, there are a number of factors that you need to consider when developing your financial plan. Legacy is much more complicated than will you leave money behind or not.

If you don't currently have an estate planning attorney, you need to hire one. I've had countless clients claim that everything was in order and their passing would not be a negative burden to the family only to find out they were completely wrong. A will used to be all that you needed to state you final wishes.

With recent regulation changes and laws passed wills are basically obsolete.

Please, even if you choose to do nothing else that I have recommended to this point, meet with an estate planning attorney to review your legal documents. The last thing your family needs while they are grieving from your passing is a legal battle trying to obtain your possessions.

Cody C. Meeks

CHAPTER 8

15 POINT
RETIREMENT CHECKLIST

So, you've made it this far! I've covered some of the areas that I see on a daily basis that could drastically affect your success during retirement. Unfortunately my grandparents didn't take action before something happened and were forced to live with the results. Since you are reading this book I'm guessing that you are just now entering retirement so for you, it's not too late! This quiz should help you determine just how prepared you are for this next leg of your journey and how protected you are in the event things don't go according to plan.

1. Within the last 10 years have you been unhappy with your investment returns?

_____Yes (2 Points)

_____Kind of (1 Points)

_____No (0 Points)

2. Does your portfolio consist primarily of stocks, bonds and/or mutual funds?

_____Yes (2 Points)

_____For the most part (1 Points)

_____No (0 Points)

3. When was the last time your financial advisor reviewed your tax return?

_____Never (2 Points)

_____Years ago (1 Points)

_____Within the last 12 months (0 Points)

4. Does your family know where to find your important documents and beneficiary forms?

_____Yes (0 Points)

_____No (2 Points)

5. Do you worry about the reliability of your retirement income plan?

_____Yes (2 Points)

_____It "should" work (1 Points)

_____No(0 Points)

6. What is your income plan during retirement?

_____I don't have one (2 Points)

_____Take 3~5% per year (1 Points)

_____My income is 100% guaranteed (0 Points)

7. Are you concerned what role the stock market performance will have on your retirement success?

_____Yes (2 Points)

_____Sometimes (1 Points)

_____No (0 Points)

8. If you died tomorrow, would your spouse be forced to live on a lower income?

_____Yes (1 Points)

_____No (0 Points)

_____I'm not sure (2 Points)

9. Do you have an emergency fund created to protect you from the unexpected?

_____Yes (0 Points)

_____No (1 Points)

10. Is your current advisor specialized to handle the unique challenges faced by retirees?

_____Yes (0 Points)

_____No (2 Points)

_____Unknown (1 Points)

11. Do you have a written budget outlining your financials during retirement?

_____Yes (0 Points)

_____No (2 Points)

12. How often do you meet with your current advisor to review your plan and make adjustments if necessary?

_____Once a year (0 Points)

_____Once in the last 2 years (1 Points)

_____It's been over 2 years (2 Points)

13. Do you know EXACTLY how much you are paying per year in fees?

_____Yes (0 Points)

_____I have an idea (1 Points)

_____I have no clue (2 Points)

14. Are you protected from a major stock market correction like we had in 2008?

_____Yes (0 Points)

_____No (2 Points)

15. Do you have updated legal documents to protect your assets and your family when you pass?

_____Yes (0 Points)

_____No (2 Points)

HOW DID YOU SCORE?

If you scored 10 or more points, there are some significant financial problems within your retirement plan and you would be the most likely to benefit from a second opinion from a qualified advisor.

If you scored 3 to 10 points, you may have the potential for risk and or issues to arise during your retirement that could affect your lifestyle or your family's when you pass. It may be wise, at this point, to seek a second opinion from a qualified advisor to make sure nothing major is at risk.

If you scored less than 3 points, more than likely you have already met with a qualified advisor and implemented their suggestions. Ultimately, you may have a few bumps in the road but you, your significant other, and your family are going to be protected. Congratulations!

CHAPTER 9

WHERE TO GO FROM HERE

With the advancement of modern medicine, a person can now expect to live nearly $1/3^{rd}$ of their life in retirement. Don't make that journey without a plan that guarantees your success!

We have covered a lot of ground in this book about common planning mistakes that could derail your success during retirement. The last and possibly the most important advice I can leave you with is to meet with a qualified advisor. Retirement is supposed to be the happiest and most rewarding years of your life. It's the only chance that you will ever get to return back to the days when you were a child. Wake up when you want to. Travel when you want to. Eat when you want to. When you're in retirement, you don't have anyone to answer to other than yourself (and possibly your spouse). Retirement is the complete freedom to do what you've always dreamed of doing. Don't let financial uncertainty hold you back. If nothing else, contact us and we'll provide you a free, no obligation review of your current situation.

It never costs you a dime to get a second opinion but will provide you the peace of mind to know that ultimately you're on the right track!

If you would like to schedule a time for us to visit, give my office a call. Our phone number is: 720-446-5595.

You can also view our website: www.financialintegrity.biz

~ To you and your retirement success, I wish you the best!

- Cody

www.ingramcontent.com/pod-product-compliance
Lightning Source LLC
Chambersburg PA
CBHW051338170526
45166CB00002B/871